SHEARSMAN
119 & 120

SPRING / SUMMER 2019

EDITOR
TONY FRAZER

Shearsman magazine is published in the United Kingdom by
Shearsman Books Ltd
50 Westons Hill Drive
Emersons Green
BRISTOL   BS16 7DF

Registered office: 30-31 St James Place, Mangotsfield, Bristol BS16 9JB
(this address not for correspondence)

www. shearsman.com

ISBN 978-1-84861-655-4
ISSN 0260-8049

Subscriptions and single copies

Current subscriptions – covering two double-issues, each around 100 pages in length – cost £16 for delivery to U.K. addresses, £18 for the rest of Europe (including the Republic of Ireland), and £22 for the rest of the world. Longer subscriptions may be had for a pro-rata higher payment. Purchasers from North America will find that buying single copies from online retailers in the U.S.A. or Canada will be cheaper than subscribing. This is because airmail postage rates in the U.K. have risen rapidly, whereas copies of the magazine are printed in the U.S.A. to meet orders from online retailers there, and thus avoid the costly transatlantic mail.

Back issues from n° 63 onwards (uniform with this issue) cost £8.95 / $16 through retail outlets. Single copies can be ordered for £8.95 direct from the press, post-free within the U.K., through the Shearsman Books online store, or from bookshops. Issues of the previous pamphlet-style version of the magazine, from n° 1 to n° 62, may be had for £3 each, direct from the press, where copies are still available, but contact us for a quote for a full, or partial, run.

Submissions

Shearsman operates a submissions-window system, whereby submissions may only be made during the months of March and September, when selections are made for the October and April issues, respectively. Submissions may be sent by mail or email, but email attachments are only accepted in PDF form. We aim to respond within 3 months of the window's closure, i.e. all who submit *should* hear by the end of June or December, although for recent issues we have sometimes taken a little longer.

The poems by Petra White in this issue first appeared in
Reading for a Quiet Morning, (Melbourne: Gloria SMH Press 2017).

This issue has been set in Bembo with titling in Argumentum. The flyleaf is set in Trend Sans.

Contents

Mary Leader

Acreage Triptych

Upon a decision by twelve of Adam's surviving grandchildren, a scant six decades after his death, to sell the 2,304.82 acres of land, for which magnitude, piece by piece by piece, Adam sacrificed every muscle and sinew, every blood vessel, any spare time and any spare change.

And when the living creatures went, the wheels went by them: and when the living creatures were lifted up from the earth, the wheels were lifted up.
            —Ezekiel 1:19

I.

A vehicle rolls
            up, stops,
                        discharges a driver,
and on occasion passengers,
            and possibly tools,
                        and possibly bags.
A vehicle, maybe a
            wagon and team.
                        A vehicle, maybe a
pickup, not called rustic.
            Rusty. Or the crowning
                        glory, a clean sedan,
just for driving to church
            on Sunday
                        and back. Each
wagon, truck, car,
            is by and by used up,
                        is sold at least for scrap
along with whatever else
            one foot in front of
                        the other got.
Barn, house, silo, tank, windmill,
            well, coop, hutch,
                        built with materials

5

dismantled and hauled from Eden,
   then maintained, mended with
      any old piece of wire
still flexible enough,
   and long enough,
      and ready to hand.

   II.

One, a littlest daughter
   of a littlest daughter, remembers,
      how "Mother" (as she came to be)
was afraid of the geese.
   A smiling matter now
      but any five-year-old
at whom a goose
   has stuck its neck straight out, and
      hissing loud, run toward
can tell
   of aggression
      and of fear.
A grandson remembers,
   as the ultimate peaceful feeling,
      hunting. Quail. Deer.
Another, who prefers silence,
   remembers how
      being taken out to cut
the young bulls did not mean
   cutting them from
      the rest of the herd but
that somebody
   young and male
      held the animal down while
a grown man seized, in one
   work-gloved hand,
      a scrotum, in the other,

6

a whetted knife, the job
                over mid-bellow, almost before
                            pain suddenly starts.
A now-bent-over granddaughter
                asks the assembled,
                            "Do you remember the big hill
west of the house
                where all the fossils are?
                            Brachiopods and Crinoids."

                III.

A stick that God whittled
                to a point, roughly,
                            in a quarter of an hour,
points. Eternities
                hence, an auction
                            that was bound to come
comes. Who
                can even know,
                            Ezekiel
having oversimplified time,
                which is the little wheel,
                            which the big,
which gear moves inside of which,
                which forms the individual unit,
                            which the span of it all?
Whatever can like wire
                be twisted
                            offers itself to the twisting.
A hand
                that has withered
                            can be stretched out to the Lord,
and as it uncurls, it points
                to the turning
                            that is next.

Sisters

Their circumstances were different,
Mary's and Sara's, because the men
they had married were different
kinds of men. By the time the rest
home became inevitable for both
these widows, Mary had plenty of
money and Sara was a pauper.
Sara was seven years the elder,
but they were built exactly alike;
by then they looked the same age;
they could be taken for twins, except
that Sara was a romantic in that she
would not even consider letting
anyone cut her almost waist-length
fine white hair while Mary, practical
and also bolder, had long since kept
her grayer and thicker hair a no-
nonsense length. Sara went into
the rest home first, and tried to keep
her dignity by ignoring the staff and
particularly by ignoring her roommate.
Happy, happy was her day when,
since Mary had to be put there too,
they could be moved into the same
room. Mary was depressed, though,
and scarcely ate. Sara, on the other
hand, rather came out of her shell,
and even went to Crafts for a while.
There, she made from a plastic
detergent bottle and a styrofoam ball
and a plastic face and a plastic wig,
a doll, and made, though her sewing
was rusty, a sweet prairie dress for
the doll and a bonnet. Besides money,
their family situations were different.
Mary's children, one of whom was

a doctor like his father, and especially
Mary's daughter, treated their Aunt
Sara as a second mother, and loved
and pitied her all the more for having
no children of her own. Even so.
When Mary's children saw their
mother going downhill fast, they
came to a decision: she would be
taken, for now anyway, to a more
expensive, much better rest home in
the town where the doctor son lived.
Aunt Sara? Well, it was welfare that
paid for her care and that was as far
as it went. Mary was in bad shape,
and for some reason it was not day
but night when they transferred her
to a gurney and rolled her out of
the room, down the hall, through
the lobby, to the waiting ambulance.
That was, in itself, an expensive way
for her to be moved from one town
to another. Sara stayed in her bed in
their room. Mary's bed was mussed,
empty. Mary had a cluster of people
around her on the gurney as it rolled,
her daughter and granddaughter
carrying her belongings, a nurse's aid
carrying the plastic ice bucket and
strawed cup that she insisted had
been paid for and should be taken,
the ambulance guy pulling the railed
gurney with one hand while holding
the I.V. bag up with the other hand,
the son signing papers at the desk,
the R.N. passing the papers to him.
Mary looked up at every face as it
came into view in this parade. She
nestled on her shoulder the doll, said

to the nurse's aid "Isn't she pretty?"
Adjusted the calico ruffle on the little
dress, adjusted the matching calico
bonnet. "Isn't she pretty?" to the
ambulance guy. Patted the calico
skirt, smoothed the calico over
the doll's flat chest. To the R.N.,
"Isn't she pretty?" To the second
ambulance guy, "Look at my dolly.
Isn't she pretty? My sister made her
for me." Every person she spoke to
smiled at her, nodding. No one,
no one was with Sara.

Michael Aiken

The ritual
(killing a forest spirit)

First: the hacksaw,
drawn in small, worn hands;
follow the lonely asphalt road
to a seasonally abandoned home.

Take the path that snakes between trees
and deep, dense gardens
to enter the Bamboo Forest:

– mystical place,
invasive church –
that cathedral of leaves,
vast rain shelter.

Next: select the victim,
the stouter the better,
and set-to along the seam of the thing
sawing…

Take him by his feet, that felled monolith,
drawn down like a serpent slowly swallowing,
branch-hands grasp desperately at friends'
as you drag him away on his back.

Haul his carcass out in the sunlight
and butcher the beast in the open,
splayed on a concrete drive:

twigs, leaves, a dismembering;
great oriental spriggan
brought low by bored children.

Last: split the body,
fracture the heart, the torso,
trunk. Grind edges of the phalanx
against plain cement, shape a speartip
never to know flesh.

Three things that remind me of home
(A Nest of Snakes)

The sea, the beach,
wildlife: bronze skinks,
sandflies,
dollarbirds and eels.
Evenings, air dense with white ants,
cockatoos cribbing on the house…

Stingless bees,
brush tails, ring tails,
blue tongues and red backs,
red bellies and browns,
little green swamp snakes alive in the laundry room,
tree frogs crowded in the crack of a stump,
sugar ants fighting back the fiercer species,
scorpions more fabled than seen…
the lost coucal pheasants and the foxes that got them
roaming bell miners
and that one lovely galah.

A sea of lantana like we live in a grotto
in some Chinese emperor's pet garden…
the blue-eyed ravens and loping currawongs
with flesh in their beaks, just spies for the invader…

tiger-striped moths swarm before a storm,
four varieties of cicada: brown drummer, black prince,
green grocer, green bottle…

butterfly chrysalises in the leaves of a white sap tree,
skinks by the millions and frogs in the drain.
Surf, nightly, rolling in through the window,
sandstone and bricks,
popping tin roof.

Such an idyll;
Where does it live on?
How?
Traffic, cats,
rats. Pigeons and exhaust.
Figs and flying foxes.

★

The beach is in my dreams again
mist-laden, like I've rarely seen it.
Separated these fifteen years or more,
together barely more than that
and yet, here it is
in my veins.

What does the life beat of a tiny bird
know of the trees that breed it,
or its parents?
Their neighbours?
Feet have been before me here
a million times and a million times longer;
is the beach in their sleep too? Their wakeful dreams?
Their living minutes?

★

The day our mother killed a snake with a spade
– severed the head in front of us kids –
we'd been collecting skinks
clustered under a plastic sheet at the top of the driveway
lazing in the sun, saving up the heat.

We cried out and she was there –
armed,
ready to go to war for us:
Okay, get ready.
Go!
We flipped the tarp and there it was,
King Brown rearing,
magnificent serpent in a mystery play
until the blade came down.

Julie Maclean

Why wives like Mrs Melville get sick of waiting

Where birds hover
         whales rise to the Doppler shift

                  He cannot hear but round the Horn
                     choirs of sperm whales blow

                     Moby and the mob swell
                        in a symphony of sonar ecstasy

                        Baleens compose foraging songs
                        as simple pings from fields of krill

                        Inside cathedrals of trill and gather
                  the she-devil calls him to heel

            but try as he might   Mister Absent and Original
      he cannot see her lips move

Cheddar Memoir
After Augustus Montague Toplady 1784-1872 and Cheddar Man

Back lanes were always
stone cold
the sun ten years away

My mother told me never
to come home
with a belly full of sperm

I ran away to a timber house
with a paling fence
I burned

in a black gloss fireplace
Whenever I returned
to a glass of sweet Jerez

assault of hyacinths
on the windowsill
at Christmas

rape of interrogation
over roast chicken
I was ready to stitch

my mouth
to become every mute
swan scrabbling

down an iced river
to get away   transmogrify
into a stalagmite

alone with the sound
of a limestone drip
coiled snake of a road

cleft of a gorge
where wild strawberries
become blood spots

between lines of the hymn
oh the guilt, the shame
but not of a cave-dwelt pagan man

Sequestering the Feeling of Grass

Once a year I cross oceans of manatee,
waterweed, frogbit—the sort of grass that
cowers under the weight of us.
I go to pull weeds from the base
of my father's tree. He hates weeds.

Weeds squat in cracked paths
like travellers and their big-eyed children,
spread unruly between geraniums,
choke drains carried by the delinquent
pigeon that tips the bird bath for the hell of it.

It never occurred to him or any of us
that the grass he so assiduously mowed
would scream at the sight of roiling blades,
that the divine smell of his tight clipped lawn,
in lines of a bowling green,
was sending out hormones of fear—
not memories of afternoons
in September when I'd come home spiked
with hay, damp patches on my jeans.

> I wanted to ask if you could see
> the wing shadowing our growing up,
> if you could bear that we weren't tidy
> or musical, like the dark cells seeding
> a requiem in the marrow of your glassy bones.
> If you could find a kind chaos
> playing your flute, arrangements
> that sometimes broke rules.

I never got to tell you that somewhere deep,
not green at all, but dry as your throat
on the last night, I feel the pain of grass
cut too short, the dying a slow brown death—
the smell of it.

Jonathan Catherall

Berlin Allergy

(after Rilke's 'Duino Elegies')

If only we too could disappear into
recognisable difference, the chains
we don't have at home, brands of toothpaste
and the pleasant confusion of S-Bahn maps.
Ich möchte ein Eis, bitte. A word like ice-
cream but not, folding itself on the tongue,
a beautiful frisson. In the partytown
of novelty, it seems you could take on
allcomers. More so when the museum
is undergoing a facelift, sections of scaffold
sheathed in metaphorical plastic, neither
historic nor ahistoric, but either.
A sheer frontalisation, an emplacement
of greying angels. You too have seen
the Wim Wenders film and so, slap
bang in the middle of Middle, we swallow
our own fluids. Every angle is terrible,
the eternal streaming service of those who
like us, take the bridge and broad parapet
as a prop for our notebook, and we, too,
only deeply reflect while away. This depth
gives us credit, which can be redeemed
at neighbouring outlets, as in the river
soap suds make photographable patterns.
For every wary animal there's a Buddha Bowl
of sweet potato, edamame, beetroot, walnuts,
salad leaves, quinoa and brown rice. What
would it be, to be able to ask rhetorical
questions to which we didn't already –
wow how cool is that so-named endlessly-
deferred-onto sprayed-on window.

Arcane Torsion Apologies

(after Rilke's 'Archaic Torso of Apollo')

Canting and unoverheard the head
of this one also already long gone,
the dick snapped off as if depriving
us of all means of kind comparison,

leaving a slightly pudgy version
with its jaundiced tinge surviving
half-hidden in the third-best exhibit
during a must-visit to the Pergamon.

Weight tilting as the meme requires
onto a single foot has sent a hairline
crack across the whole from hip

diagonal to massy hip and the fine
work of pinning, unseen, mires
the viewer reluctantly in stasis.

Cant 1

& honestly didn't go down to the boats
which were all chained anyway & flaky
and popped on a black and white filter
                                        the sea
smeared with traces of tar & hubris
26 likes on a good day

maritime theme & the ooze of time
                        jugged heat   aroma of incense
            jaguar purr & lynx-sweat
& breton tops a roaring trade   on margate sands

        getting everywhere   into your nikes into
the sandwiches   here's one I made earlier   & here's
one with HDR
                    man   I dig the ell-square pitkin
& bring out the shades   'wotcha'
        said david williams blonde & squarejawed at ten & a spurs fan
excellent sausage rolls
                        singing fantasy island
the insides warm   on the massive
                                        for that time
                                            telly
        & his whole family when the tiresias o.g.
            screaming and hugging
                                        layers stacked on lairs
                                        bods in the azure air
                                        grit in the
oysters

Cathy Dreyer

Ewelysses

For Tom Clucas with apologies to Alfred, Lord Tennyson

If I am Queen of all the Kindly Bred
I rule these barren crags to little end.
Rams come, rams go, their services distract
Me briefly, then it's back to collop spats –
Which ewe was ewsed to graze which heft? (Or not.)
They hoard, and sleep and feed, and never think
To ask how I got here to this small field.
I roamed the world beyond these leys, beyond
These dry-stone walls. My deeds inspired the bards.
Sometimes the fates dispatched me quite alone
Sometimes I led a fearless flock, a bold
And brave brigade whose hearts I held and who
Held mine through storms whipped up by gods and men,
Across the wildest ponds and greenbelt lands,
Exotic suburbs where we dined with theaves
And bought strange tinctures from illegal stands.
Oh yes! We tasted riot's heady drench
And always my bell wethered at the front.
Far on the pealing streets of brassy Bath
From where I saw the wool of lands beyond,
And spun and wove a tapestry of proud
Tomorrows with fresh woods and pastures new.
How are the mighty hefted. You have found
Me broken-mouthed on claughty soil, confined,
Riggwelted, in a barren hirsel's scope.
Provincial nickerings of rams and lambs
Are satisfying ruminations for
The mutton-hearted. But I am brave.
Yes! Underneath my dagged and frizzy coat
This gray spirit burns with hot desire
For sorting races to the heftless stars
Beyond the utmost bound of sheepish thought.

They took my sons, each sweet Telemachus.
There's nothing I can say of that blackloss.
Besides, I have no crook or field to will.
Some gimmer not-yet-born will take my realm
Of cairns and dung-specked grass beneath the clouds
When I am drafted down to gentler fields.
To her will fall the task of mustering
The flock to march from here or there, from up
The field to meadowlands below and back
Again, because we need fresh grass, because
The weather's worsened or improved, because
We're due at our *al fresco* salon for
The season's new look cut 'n blow-dry style,
Or because the dog has teeth. It's boring and
Demanding. I won't grieve my stony throne.

On cloudless nights the lights of motorways
Could guide me down to town, from where I
Would escape concealed inside a truck and jolt
The dark, broad roads to distant parts to find
My followers, the flock that battled by
My side (without a thought for grazing rights
Which might accrue through customary ewes
And family association with a pitted field).
They took the rough, cold winds and boiling
Sun without a bleat, nor whined of hunger
In austerity, or moaned of injury on walks.
I'm almost cast and for the cull, but I dream
Still of great travails, of winning once again
The grace and favour of the gods with nerve
And grit preserved in fleece. Before the darkness
Shuts my eyes, before the calls of missing
Lambs return to block my ears, let me round up
The ewes of yore, and gather too my wits
And let us lift our noses to the air, forget
Our bursenbellies one last rambunctious time.
It's not too late to seek a better world,
Set off and, trotting two-by-two, eschew
Our wool-lined furrow; for my purpose holds

To find a lunky through the crumbling walls
And roam beyond the limits of the farm
And meet the famous Mary and Bo-Peep.
Our three bags are not bursting full, and they
May need repairing. But our spirits knit
To glatter what's reduced by time and fate.
We meet the moment with unbratted will
To graze the verge and not stray into fields.

Pa'ing It Forward

Dad says that
I
must be
careful
that men can't
stop once the point of no return has been surpassed there is no
control it's simple physiology the relaxation of smooth muscles
in the sponge-like regions of erectile tissue their transmitters
spewing nitric oxide from deflaccidating caverns to commence
tumescence not forgetting acetylcholine which helps to regulate
the NO a NO that's stronger than a woman's NO it roars into
the sponge-like regions of erectile tissue increasing intracellular
guanosin monophosphate in great waves decreasing calcium ionized
of course to relax the sponge-like regions of erectile tissue aided
by the cyclic adenosin monophosphate pathway turned on by
intercellular emissaries from neural or cryptoparacrinal sources
including prostaglandins also a variety of phosphodiesterase
enzymes inactivate the cyclic nucleotides thereby limiting their
erectogenic action which is another reason why   '
Dad says that
I
must be
careful

On the Triumph of Artifice

i.m. Veronica Forrest-Thomson

Let the word be a finger pointing at the moon.
And please, do, look at the moon. I'll be with Veronica,
looking at the word.
She says she "shall turn to Mr Hughes'
Crow and his justification for thrusting
it down our throat." (I'm flattered
that she wants to share a throat with me.)
Vee says: "Nothing escapes Mr Hughes; nothing could escape," [naughty!].
She goes on, eventually, to a soaring eagle from *Crow and the Birds*,
Vee says, as she runs Hughes through with her vorpal
sword: "These lines are not going to break the bank
at Monte Carlo but they are not bad; they
give us a glimpse of what Mr Hughes' talent
might have led him to, if he also had not fallen
victim to the stance of 'visionary'."
And here's a bit more "Crow", she crows, quoting
a line full of *panties* and adding:

"We are reminded of Eliot's *Sweeney*
Agonistes:
                    You'd be bored.
          Birth, and copulation, and death."

Veronica has this to say: "We are bored,
very bored indeed when all the work
of intellect or hand, all the complexity
of human dealings with language
and the world, is reduced to presenting
such statements literally."
Oui. Let us hug the sound.

The poem draws on Chapter 5 of *Poetic Artifice* by
Veronica Forrest-Thomson [Shearsman Books, 2016].

Simon Perchik

It's easy – you wait for these leaves
to finish feeding, pick clean this soft scarf
dropped unopened on the ground

– it's then you can lean over
the way this branch gathers around
though each death still hides behind

what the wind looks like
when you take hold the same day each year
and jump face down for the landing.

★

Though you say nothing about the road north
these curves strike back, make one breath
take longer than the others to begin and end

as the migratory route all stone follows
reaches the horizon without moving
– in such a silence you dead

never had a chance, are held in place
to be pulled out the ground as the shadow
you need to say goodbye, letting it fall

still alive into each stream that left
for the open sea, already smelling from salt
and the small stones to be swallowed whole.

★

It's your usual wound :one day each year
gaping from under the ground as some flame
sure it can stay lit alone, won't need this

half glass, half still circling down
listening for the smoke making room
by relying on you to stay

and with barely enough string
weep, make the rescue, let the fire go out
on its own and hour by hour each separation

become one year heavier, harder
though the dead still meet in a near-by grove
marked off the way each calendar is at home

clinging to branches covered with leaves
in rows to help you remember where
it keeps the horizons, when to look around.

★

Just a shoe, unlaced, left on the floor
near the one you wear to bed
making sure you stay awake

where there should be two – are trembling
with tears from each mouth
all night calling to the other – you start

the limping side to side as a wound
waiting to be brought closer
held tight, make the bed stop.

★

You trust this rotting flower box
the way a bed-sheet is folded back
makes its home in the same room

the dead hear as corners and fingertips
– there's time and though it's not raining
you cover her grave with your hand

as a promise, say nothing about
why there are no flowers where the ground
is shaded – in such a silence

what you reach for rises from your arms
as arms, one around the other
now that this dirt is empty.

Claire Crowther

Think Workers in Energy Futures

The ship of our time is no tree
with a yard arm, a mast. No walnut shell rocks us home.

Planes charge across skies, leaves blowing
away from the branch. But we two travel water-earthed

in this swaying skyscraper of a carbon-saver.

We think
We think and talk
We talk of thoughts

We – what workers are this we –
think – what work is not thought –

Whose thought crosses:
    hours with days
    power with energy
    means with ends

Outside, a feral surface.
It hisses apart for our ship   seething and soothing
    the dry soles   that walk our way.

One of us
    meditates
on how to demonstrate linkage
    repeatableconsistentreproducedoverandover.

Another remarks on the glory of coincidence:

'Is sun gold
because, of all its photons,
golden ones
are the most plentiful?

28

Causal connection
or coincidence?'

'Coincidentally,
the energy of a golden photon
is just right for a solar cell
to operate most efficiently.'

Margins, curled
gingerly between light and hydropower,
run
till horizons claim the sun.

Sunbeat

Don't we feel the natural sound of sun beating inside itself as any
human body beats?

Don't our atoms measure disruption into unexpected lines or graphs
as we float on?

Do we take ourselves to heart and resonate?

Are we all Antarctic ice sheets cracking in weakening heat, singing
under strain?

Surely the sun gives us our physic.

John Levy

How Diane Arbus Would've Photographed Me

Say she happens to be in Tampa when my
family is staying at a hotel there. Summer of
'58, which makes me
six or seven. She's out by the hotel

pool. She likes pools, just as she likes beaches
and nudist camps. She positions herself
near the steps in the shallow end as I begin to
climb out. Surprised by the fully-clothed woman

with a big black camera around her neck I
stop, one foot on a higher step, water dripping down my face,
thin arms drooping at my sides. I have my mouth open
for that first photo, the one

she exhibits, as I look
into her camera
with no thought in my head that I should do
anything with the face I forget all about.

Another Letter to Paul Matthews

Dear Paul,

Yesterday morning I was raking a path
in our yard when a Cooper's Hawk

landed on a branch about 10 feet away
and level with my eyes. We were both

in the shade.
As the saying goes, time

seemed to stop. The radiant yellow claws and legs
of the hawk on the branch

and its
one yellow eye with a black pupil

met mine. I've never had a hawk land so close.
Noise seemed to cease. I stopped

moving. It
was still. And then I was me again, holding the rake,

outside doing a chore when I wanted to also be
inside, trying to write. So,

30 seconds of motionless
what? Wonder, on *my* part? Amazement? Magic?

I moved my rake knowing
the hawk would leave. And it did. Flew

to a higher branch, a little further off
and then I started raking again and it

flew into our neighbor's yard. Should I have
stood there

with it (although that "with" only
applies to me because I can't imagine

what preposition the
hawk would use if it spoke English

and wanted to get picky
about prepositions, but I doubt

it would choose "with" and also
I wonder what sort of accent it would have).

Should I add (in my defense?)
that I had been out in the heat and

humidity for about 30 minutes
at that point, whereas I'd told myself

I'd rake the path for 15 minutes
tops

before returning to my TO DO list, which,
probably unlike anyone else's

in my neighborhood (let's call my
neighborhood a five mile radius

in any direction) had
Poems

at the top of the list. And I do like writing
first thing, so to speak, after breakfast.

Had the hawk already eaten?
If the hawk could both speak and write English.

and also wrote a TO DO list
each morning, what are the chances

it would have at the top of the list
LAND NEAR A HUMAN?

Anyhow, Paul, here it is, the next day.
You and I

often write each other about seeing
birds. You with your occasional eagles.

I don't know if you'd have

stayed longer with the hawk. I suspect
you would have. Maybe you'd have

gone home and started a painting
and finished it then photographed it

and sent it to me. I don't imagine
you would've joked

about what preposition the hawk
would've fussily

settled upon to describe its
proximity to *your* eyes. I do imagine

you would've done justice to its
yellows

and everything else it brought
to that branch. Your painting

would've said silence
too.

DS Maolalaí

Writer's block

she said
she took three short showers a day
and her housemate
took a long one
once a week

"so we balance out
sort of.

it's almost like
we're one
normal person."

she cooked really
well
and fucked
really
well
and had an apartment
with a view of the stadium nearby
rising out of houses
like a pot of geraniums.

she worked
in some tech thing
and read cheap books in paperback
and loved tv
and meals
in expensive restaurants.

she didn't write poetry
or paint
or make music. so different

to all the other girls I'd loved.
I loved her anyway.
she was easy
to love
and be around
and she never asked for more of me
than whatever I had in my pocket.

I loved her.
and being with her
made me write
so
badly

Terror House

I sent some poems
to this magazine;
terror house
in budapest. they were,
I thought,
quite good. really
raw
heart as a muscle
type stuff. I'd read a couple of pages
before I sent them in
and it all seemed
pretty similar
to what I do. so I was confident
already
and then they took 3.

it was only after
they went up
that I found out
the editor

was that Matt Forney cunt — one of those
alt-right
nazi-type guys. jesus
fuck. that took my wind
right down.
I wrote him that night
and asked to have them taken down;
that it was nothing personal
but their whole philosophy
repulsed me. I would have gone harder
but I'm a coward
and listen:
they still had my email.

he was actually
very gracious about it.
got them off
right away. I'm still listed as an author though
on the site
and it's the second time
that's happened to me.
what is it
about honest,
straight
and personal stories
that makes them appeal so much
to fucks like that?

Kerry Featherstone

Jonathan and Carl at the Battle of Maldon

Four battles with the Vikings
on the coast that year.
Silently on the Blackwater came two or three thousand
to the Northey Island Causeway,
and the Essex men went out to fight them,
where the maps show mean high water.

And one March morning a millennium later
Jonathan and Carl went out to read *The Battle of Maldon*
in that place.
They looked out over the shire and
studied the ways,
for the number 75 via Colchester Zoo does not run on Sundays.
And for this they cursed Regal Busways.
Of Chelmsford.

Only God knows
what the milita saw as they allowed the enemy to crowd closer.
Their leader so sure of his manhood that
he gave them a foothold on the narrow beach.
He showed them how to hold a weapon, weight a spear:
so they fought.
"Thought the harder, heart the keener, courage the greater as our
    strength faileth."
But the chief was already dead.
And the poet says "Only God knows who at the end shall possess
    this fight's field."

And Jonathan took Carl by the hand
past the football ground,
down South House Chase
to Furthersea Field.
And Jonathan began to read as they looked over

the causeway to Long Marsh.
But Carl proved soft for the coming battle, and at line 98
in which the Northmen cross the shining water shore,
said firmly "I need to pee".
And Jonathan kept on: "Thought the harder, heart the keener..."
But Carl, like Ethelred, was unready, and would have paid Danegeld
for the onslaught to stop.
And he said "I'm busting".
And Jonathan closed the book with a slap and said
"Christ, Carl, it's not always about your cock!"

Who at the end can possess the fight's field?
The surface needs to be broken before
we can tell the full tale:
between the centre circle and the changing names
might be more stories than a plough can find.
The battle left no trace
of young men finding their death on the Blackwater,
or of the pages flapping
back in the wind to a world when
love between them needs
great courage and a heart that is keen.

Lear Masala at Watermead

Human skulls, auroch bones and cooking stones
tell when food was steamed here.
And Lear. Water-man, sea-god, ruling freshwater in England's myth,
super-fluvium Soram.
Cutting through kingdoms with his daughter's blade.
Some say Cordelia loved her father just as salt,
and at this Lear cried. And they lie
under the stream's vault.
So the Britons said Kaerleir, but the Saxons said
Leicester, because everything is named as it changes hands.

* * *

Lear slept as the slim Soar was canalled
and pinked with cloth dye.
The next digging was sand and gravel, building a city
the colours of turmeric, paprika, okra.
And then came to walk around wide-skirted meads.

* * *

Meanwhile in the Mahabharata, Yayatis asks his children
"who will face death for me and keep me young?"
And Puru, the youngest, steps towards old age.
After a thousand years, Daddy is ready to accept that his
acquisitions of gold, girls and armies are not worth
a fenugreek,
and so the two are saved.
And this is the seed of Lear...

* * *

Now Belgrave looks up from the epics
of grandparents,
and walks around a lake or two
(daal and dosas in tiffin boxes keeping the mix fresh).
And later in the story
the poet Dirgatama has a prayer
to the divine doctors and he says:
"may the turning of the days not tire me,
may the fires not burn me,
may I not bite the earth,
may the waters not swallow me."

* * *

A little black dog barks at the plastic mammoth,
the waves blow and the platform shudders
with a King's grief.
(Celtic sea-god of the old days better than any plastic mammoth).

Cordelia shakes the holy water from her heavenly eyes,
into the lake of darkness.
"May the turning not tire me,
fires not burn me,
waters not swallow me."
A love like salt, cutting through history's masala.

David Rushmer

What Space Between Us

language

    a stone

    total

weightlessness

    attachment

    the circle
        one becomes

violence

    I was the object

the anguish of disappearing

pain of our speech

The Way

from the unfurling

       ignition of wings

the wind
       takes our breath away

waiting   for the sky
       to remove its mask

       exhale into stone
time buried in its folds

muscle of earth
       showing its scars

the body's imprint

Petra White

The Lovely Sphinx

She knows already he will solve her riddle: she must dash
herself against the rocks, all her lovely parts,
the supple lion legs whose fur she combed and kept so bright,
her woman head, her crackling dragon wings,
princely gleaming teeth,
gently webbed fingers, delicate brown nails,
a puckered and mottled green torso,
naked and soft as an infant's, her sprightly odour
of raspberries and almonds.
The riddle, so perplexing
it kept the city free of men
whose minds were not fine.
Their bodies piled around her, she killed them
with a jet of blood from her heart,
poisonous to all who walk on two legs.
Now Oedipus stands before her,
squat, young, bald,
all the blather comes out of his mouth.
I will defeat you, give me your riddle,
I killed a man on my way here, don't mess with me.
She sees his fate in a snap.
In a moment of motherly compassion
is tempted to withhold the riddle.
But he leans in closer, he seethes into her teeth
Give. Me. The. Riddle!
Then in a breath he solves it.
The blood jet bubbles and sears in her chest.
She watches him run off, squawking with glee.
I solved the riddle! The city is mine! Where is the princess?
What now, she wonders. Must I?
My life is only just beginning.
She sees Death coming to escort her to the cliff.
He is a man with eyes of tedious fire.
She smiles at him. Answer my riddle.

Oedipus Walking

Then then then.
Happiness kicks itself.
His narrative starts and he can't stop it.
He walks as a donkey walks
through villages and streets.
Nothing can get any worse,
his eyes are glutted with darkness.
It swims all around him and glitters
with tiny stars. He will never run out of it.
His blind eyes shed tears, warm and weak like bathwater.
The homeless night. How to grasp
the self that has half-killed itself.
One step then another.
There were moments
when he owned them, happiness and hope.
Twin songs like twin goats
curling round his knees.
Mother-wife, sister-daughter, hold them close.
He tries to marshal his sorrow.
Oh sweet song of doom, go over there, stand next to me,
stand above me.
Where is the sea, where is the forest
where I was left to die. Find the beginning,
the baby ankles pinned together.
If they had not listened, would it still have come true?
Voices against the railing. Oedipus, Oedipus.
Let them in.
He tries to order his sorrow which stretches
from his umbilical cord to his bald adult head,
to his pitchforked eyes.
What order can he put it in?
The future spits past at him.
So he treads along the earth,
further and further towards the beginning
of the beginning of the beginning
shut in his mother,

shut in his future wife,
when he was nothing but potential
and all the potential was blighted and sick,
all his blood hingeing on the words of the seer.
And the seer, a quiet man in a quiet room
wearing necklaces of fates.

Jocasta

Just an eagle I was, following its prey,
swooping here and there, hooking and embracing –
one thing led to another
and another.
Things happened to me,

I did not make anything happen.
Each day I tie a new noose
out of silk, out of rope.
I would hang myself as I am intended to.
Yet if my son survives to push through time so I should.

My eyes bounce off the day, off the lake
off the walls and ceilings.
There is nothing I can see that is large enough
to unsee that has gripped me.
A life stuffed under my eyelids.

Not a minute can be ironed out straight.
No second of joy retrieved.
What sort of woman I am.
Not a mother, not a wife,
in between,

hot and searing
yet cold to the touch
hard like steel
that death cannot taste
as it beckons me every day.

A thing that was happened to.
I gather myself up,
and practise making things happen.
I make the servants march and live
when they want to die at my feet.

I make the tiny dark stars inside me scatter.
Days and days to exist
only time kills me now.
Time, my guest.
I make nothing happen and it happens.

Peter Robinson

Return to Sendai
for Miki Iwata

Beyond a rusted, padlocked gate
at Matsunami-cho
where for years I'd wait and pine,
under its branches' long wave curve
what with the Lawsons convenience store
and local supermarket gone,
it's really like there's no such zone.

Beyond the rusted, padlocked gate
at Matsunami-cho
where our flat-block's since demolished,
although you say those lines of mine
have a place in the place's history,
I'm far too old to clamber over.
It's like those fourteen years had been abolished.

Beyond this rusted, padlocked gate
at Matsunami-cho
a risen sun would alter all
moving across its scuff-marked parquet,
souvenirs of elsewheres on each wall.
Here two daughters came to life,
and we played 'nothing but blue skies' in the dawn.

Beyond that rusted, padlocked gate
at Matsunami-cho
we've been exiled from our exile
under the pine wave's broken curve,
and pushing through rucked, buckled asphalt
even here the summer grasses
show deep-buried traces –

like those verses of mine from some thirty years ago.

At Slader's Yard

for David Inshaw

There's a corrugated-iron roof,
its undulations flattened
by settled years of lime-green moss;

it juts into repurposed space
where stone-wall textures are revealed,
enhanced by sparser finishes,
framed pictures hung against it:

a dusk cloud risen behind its hill,
the portrait of one tree in moonlight,
another strafing seagull …

they emphasize the edges
letting on bare sail-loft opposite:
a dried grey wood interior
where all the thrifty meanings start.

Then, me too, I'm a counter of clouds
come over the hills like this one
'salmoning' in a 'deepening blue';

they fill up turning windscreen glass
(you see I've put the car in too)
above West Bay's horizon

with a borrowed sharpness, focus
from promptings given by
that pink house under its precipitous cliff.

Recounting them, you're at least alive to
how this word-cloud builds and disperses
ideas like a Nordau's or Lombroso's –

and how they're clouds themselves, these verses.

Weymouth Sands

'I shrink to seek a modern coast
Whose riper times have yet to be…'
—Thomas Hardy

There's a great, white apparition far up ahead
with art-deco wings and a central tower;
you wonder what it might have been,
ask passersby, who've no idea.
Yet how its intrigue draws us on
till, aquamarine, the trim's grown clear
and a name: RIVIERA HOTEL
in the glass of that central tower –
the scene or setting for a *noir* whodunit,
a *crime passionnel* overlooking Weymouth Bay.

Returning, now, towards its town
(the clocks gone back today)
sunburst spokes of rays, you see,
are flecked about with wisps of cloud,
the turquoise, pink and purple
patches in a vast display –
as if the sunset's scene or setting
were *practised*, too, *in the art of deception*
and it could take that *need* of his
for ways back to their *want* as well …

With lights come on across the town
so much is coming to an end
(though we're not yet aware) –
as if Thomas Hardy in his 'Invitation' poem
had really recommended them
to take on some antiquity,
when in that land of theirs
(as he could well have known),
oh no, they'd not get free
from the patriotic gore, dripping tears of its own.

But now wave-facets in a dusk-lit swell
slope and slop around this shore.
Silhouetted, apparitions turn
homeward in the crepuscule;
and under lamps' intervals, down this promenade,
who'll recall memorials
for the dead GIs of Slapton Sands
in Hardy Country, more than sixty-years back now?
and though, us too, the sun gone down,
we're as reluctant to go
seeking out a modern coastline,
their experience, can't I count on it as mine?

Ruth McIlroy

Theme [
exhaust]

I have reduced my price to free me

there was something exhausted
there was mistaken

flee the mine it is exhausted
flee the dead horse

the opal has fallen out of my ring
it was a catastrophe I keen and laugh

and it was important precious
gone finger empty for the miracle

A charm with Yarrow

I will choose yarrow and yarrow will delight my elegant fingers
    warmer

my lips are the juice of six strawberries, in the sea I am an island
and on the land I am a hill and when the moon disappears, I am a
    star

and I am a staff to you when you are weak, and my lips are warmer
    and warmer
and I can love a bird out of a tree and I choose yarrow yarrow.

after A Charm with yarrow (Scottish Gaelic, traditional folk charm)

Aims of the Zoos Questionnaire's Survey

The first question ('Name of zoo:' and 'Country:')

Question 2 ('What diet (food & nutrients)
do you feed the aardvarks in your zoo?')

Question 2a ('Do you sometimes feed them food scraps
(as sometimes pigs are fed with)?')
Question2b ('How do you feed the food?') was asked
in the hope that some zoos would use a fake termite-mound.

Question 3 ('What seems to be the purpose?')
should then help to understand why aardvarks swim at all.

Dubrovnik

I walk unsheltered through the Old City
cleansed of mercy terrified loving

high and innocent, the cathedral walls
are pocked with delicate marks of shells

there has been artillery on this town;
the city has been loosened from its soul

which slipped out through the Vrate Gate
and made its way across the burning hills

a heart will also slip out through a gate
and what is left eats bitterness.

Amlanjyoti Goswami

Disobedience
(After Paul Celan)

They will ask you your name. They will ask you, they will ask you
Till they no longer want to know.
Till vultures circling the cold night air,
Tire of their flying.
Till cold hearts find something colder than
This vast indifferent universe.

Fight not, son, they are many, we few,
And they will blame you for fighting,
And find a reason for their blame.
No one will ever come to help, no one
Will come to save you.

I will not go out mother I will not see the stars tonight
Not look at the moon that is my blessing.
The walls of the night are cold. Outside, it rains
A sudden storm, a hard heavy rain that knows no end.
The night grips my fist, it calls me awake, though my eyes are closed
And they have forgotten what waking meant.

Above me is the tree with juicy guavas, where we once played.
    Green as pulp.
Above the chilling words of justice, calling out to every bone.
Above those little men and women, who fought a weary fight alone.
Above, the tall television tower where the news is never born.

And where do I go, tonight, mother?
The doors of the heart are barred. Even the faithful have found
A way to depart.
I am brave they say, I am brave
To hear the silence that stalks this land.

Brave to call out to thunder: where are you, tonight?
Brave to see the light not the fire.

I wanted to obey you, mother, but life called me away,
And beyond life, the still shrill quiet of beyond, that no one
Sees from here. Beyond the glitter of the furthest stars,
Beyond forever. It is there forever was born, it is there
Forever stays
looking for a dwelling.

A god grieving

When Karna fell,
A passing soldier asked: Why?
Why didn't the better archer win?
And by far, the better man.

This isn't just.

Another, smoking a chillum,
Dead of night,
The blood dry:

That would change nature's wheels.
Imagine Krishna, driving the chariot, with no Arjun
Into the crowd of battle,
We would all make way,
But a god grieving?

How could humankind survive
a god grieving?

Going to College

Stranded
Gates of logic.
Time flies, fires in the hearth lie unstoked.
Lucky to be standing here still,
While thoughts stray – disciplines,
Border crossings.

A life of one's own, is lonely.
A drowsy afternoon, deserted library
Fluttering a gust of wind
At page 37.

In a study of spices, for example,
Kitchen smells
From lands camel-bound,
The disciplines mingling
The law looking away.

Vik Shirley

never been to volkovo
from Dostoyevsky's 'Notes from Underground', translated by Natasha Randall

ten

inexorable pleasure //
      among the dandies //
gentleman do you know // the main point //
           of my spitefulness //
    utter filthiness // scaring sparrows in vain //
i may foam at the mouth //
bring me // some kind of dolly // to play with //
      my soul might soften //
contrary elements // teaming within me //
      not on purpose // they tortured me //
       to the point of shame //

twenty-two

flog yourself // as painfully as you can //
      these bloody insults //
this mockery //   the groans of an educated man //
   coarse *muzhik* //   sort of nastily viscous //
    futilely straining //
  irritating // himself and others //
a half-*kopeck* piece //
    the roulades and the capers //
out of malice /// sensuality lies //
     feel it yourself // every minute //
    a *chenapan* //
my despicable groans // now //
    an even more awful roulade //

sixty-three

my revenge // most simple // most genius //

nevsky at four o'clock //

       innumerable torments //
       humiliations // outpourings of bile //

   darted around like carp //
              in-between // passers by //
convulsive pain // heat in spine // *misère* // of attire //
       darting little figure //
     nasty obscene fly // more clever // more cultured //
more noble // than everyone //
                that is a given //

eighty-two

this stain alone // would subtract nine tenths //
    of my personal merit //
          I knew it was very base //
time for reality // monstrously exaggerating //
what was there to do //
      zverkov would greet me //
that dullard trudolyubov //   little insect //
    snigger // worm himself into //
      abjectness of vanity //
shrunk away // shrunk away //
         in powerful paroxysms //
of my fever //
    I dreamed of gaining the upper hand //

Jazmine Linklater

Mine

'But his wife looked from behind him, and she became a pillar of salt'

With my pickaxe I excavate you
Part by part by part

Chop out your heart & deseed you
for planting   to coax into life again
like a fire

★

I molten me
tip into moulds
for the cooling

★

How you swelled up & captured
every detail imaginable
how you shrank again
retaining it all

★

I roll your amber & tsavorite organs
over my seal   see your story

One panorama loops
thousands of moments
without beginning or end or colour

Compressed, there's no scattering
light, no sky

★

Not white

Not blue

★

Bones of steel & ceramic
but clouds weep
for your glittering asphalt
& your flesh become liquid
undrinkable

★

You dissolve you
evaporate part
leave behind nothing
more than a tear-mark

(Her Salt) or, The First Mermaid

I.

There she lies on the gallery floor, in pieces. Illusion of solidity. The eyes of her bones peer at your looking in ceramic & steel. She's all offcuts. Residues. Parts. She almost always isn't & she wants you to know it: surface still glitters a hundred electrical clichés though you plucked her smooth, ground down her feathers to powder & bottled dried sea-foam, compressed it tight to make lightless. Rolled horizons in multiple: melting mist into solid & preserved in dry air, denying all possibility still inside her of liquid, dissolve.

II.

You wanted her stacked, a column dressed in a tight sheath, arms out at right angles. Like the altar that floats & moves in the water. Almost camouflaged here on the concrete, she disobeyed you again: lay down in protest in pieces, in the undergrowth, kitchen, desert and forest. We're eating; we're looking. Doves & fish. Price lists & storage solutions. It rains: her flanks rise & fall with the weight of the atmosphere: residual music sings the kuliltu in moisture; sword in, right up to the hilt.

Norman Jope

Celluloid Is Colder Than Love

Night footage of the red-light zone. Whores with umbrellas, in a million-person village at the heart of Europe, patrol an edge-land like a frieze from a Sumerian tomb. There are showrooms and oil-spattered workshops, whores positioned at hundred-metre intervals like marker posts on a journey to Tartarus. The footage of the edge-lands continues for what seems like hours, but it's only for seconds.

The killer prowls in his extravagant hat. Murder, for him, is a kind of purification and he has something of a Bavarian Pinky Brown to him, the same self-righteousness turned sour. In contrast, the Director is flabby and thuggish, a machine that chews up cigarettes… only his playful walk beside the canal is at all endearing and this, too, culminates in an act of slaughter that is as instinctive as it is futile.

The three of them – the Director, the killer whose name is Bruno and Johanna, bouffant-haired and languid, in the mid-yawn of her life – live from one act of nihilism to the next. As the Director returns to the other side of the lens, Bruno and Johanna push a trolley through the Wirtschaftswunder's blandishments… sneaking a bottle of schnapps or a tin of calf's brains into their capacious pockets.

So where does the red road lead? It leads to a getaway through featureless countryside, the killer (unaccountably betrayed by Johanna) lying dead and fish-eyed on the pavement where his carcass was thrown. Johanna confesses and the Director absolves her with a single word – the word is Whore, which is what she knows she is. Only the sky retains its innocence, by fading to whiteness like the garb of a ghost.

Self-Portrait As Franz Walsch

Eat snails and you become one. I stuck to my original order of meatloaf and egg... my tastes are that simple, whether I disguise them or not.

You could claim me as a Stoic even though women are drawn to me in the strangest of places. A waitress strokes my hair lovingly as we dance to the juke-box. A porn-peddling waif from Transylvania propositions me on the midnight tram. My brother's girlfriend undresses me like a doll and I barely move a muscle.

It was clear from the start that I could play the role of the unmoved mover – my sheer indifference to the richness of life invested me with a dodgy charisma. My brother lay dead on the floor as I entered the undecorated apartment and all I could do was pat his arm lightly.

My former mistress plots my destruction with a chisel-faced cop. He wilts in front of the wall-sized street map as his superior aims to nail me for my brother's demise. My current mistress is innocent, good-hearted and takes out loans she cannot afford to keep me in meatloaf and egg and posters of King Ludwig II.

That wallpaper street-map is the two-dimensional world I inhabit, the Mappa Mundi of my crippled existence. The city it depicts is a rat-maze by the name of München, city of the beer-hall putsch and the Swan King's madness.

Only the Gorilla – everybody has to have a name he says – is reliable but he, too, obeys superior orders. The order he took to kill my brother was one I had to respect (after all, he sang).

My own death awaits in a deserted supermarket – 'Cobbler, stick to your last' is my Rosebud finale - and I know that my current mistress, with her demented dreams of our settling down to a delicatessen or a magazine delivery service, will soon get over me. And that my former mistress will weep at my grave, despite her role in digging it, and tell the world how much she loved me.

But I was pulp from the very beginning, bored with all of it, taking refuge in nonsense songs on a scratchy gramophone. And soon the animals will have all fallen silent, my demise as sad as Sinbad's, my world-line a skid-mark left by the collision of a dog-turd and a passing foot. Not that I'll reject your compassion, if you have any to spare.

Note: these pieces are inspired by two of Rainer Werner Fassbinder's early films, namely *Love is Colder than Death* (*Liebe ist kälter als der Tod*) and *Gods of the Plague* (*Götter der Pest*).

Peter Larkin

Spaces | | In the Way of Forest *(Extract)*

Pathless betweens no solitary dressage but pined into tall separation

if firs lean off firs they are not countervailing a forest rearing but will rake (rank) its defacing | | a full plight of forest is least chasm for trees

with no issuing spatiality other than aggregation, apposition, forest result

spaces which can't be postponed even in their inert givens | | at forest collide with fully operational make-way trees

a small circuit stretches into belonging (along lengths) | | screened into its own spaces, events between its own orifices

whereabouts between mysterious (elongated, discontinuous) cresting | | are these betweens entirely under cover?

no change of mass in the interspaces apart from falling seeds | | in every nearer interval of the untorn

to say spaces in touch are climbing a trunk at a time | | refining, breathing its horizontal concessions, the relinquishment entirely upright

latent spaces between where forest is abandoned, unrandomed, slyly adorned

in which there is no gradation of trees but sliding positions of a forest attending to distinctions of scope | | whose adjustments are now ferried in root, unqueued as green gap

deep weather-lane into trees, a tandem to allegory | | a gap gone
astray but not pierced, as such remains every incomplete tree

almost a spiral of light but etiolated by gaps in the vertical, embeds a
forest's exception to spread

inhabited spears of tree or small peduncles cherishing what the gaps
haven't deserted | | there was never any freer void to assert

great surfaces of a wood run entirely through its pauses, subside as
immensely relayed

cohabits forecasting woodland interval | | no longer simply amid
but a whole spatial weather of sheltered surface

a forest's prayerful pitch is along the interim beside it, a species out
of hiding

no summitism here apart from room for empty clefts | | side on side
of each others' tangents of division, touch the inter-domain

small gains of copse towards every carrying passage | | steep borders
transmit until lightly vertical | | accompany layout off the dial of
the neutral

forests get supervened on, their subscenes inventories of passage
minus any clear break-through | | a space is not a lair, lays open how
it is every envoy quietening the relay

defended but not offended at a vapour of cover | | spaces suspend
any alike-forest oasis of minimal (infinitive) exchange

overcome by elsewhere already overgone here, passing an intimate
through an unclose

as trees puncture the open, seal its injects with denser bowers | | and
still the space scours, but exactly in terms of

a mass of space compromised by a missing map of trees | | canopy
has retextured its offload grid | | space is up against (collates) its own
artifices of distribution | | forest rides will withhold any naturality
of retribution

spaces in the forest pitch a vacant platform of duress | | trees heal
this distress of penetration | | they lend their vertical fenestrations
unaggrieved

a range of dearth exceeding its depiction in trees, each departure
thickens the furtherance | | or nearer as an incoming of segment
(place) arrives on frame, spatial shell

leeway is the frail consumer, traces assuming an advantage of covert
| | no entry will manage such a reciprocal exit | | the way out has
a longer history than passage

lanes through trees are not the forest's line of flight | | set linear
at integral microfret, leaves across a foiled avenue | | of all places a
world unhugely available | | forest spaces only half-gone but entirely
given on

a ground of trees in diminishing may shunt inclusion onto forest
supplement | | deeper incursion once branches tread into | | a shelf
of foliage has committed its own intersect

as if one wood could be seen from another across a paltry interval | |
one that leaves them both to their own convergences

what self-stealing in nature is swept up at a ruse of trees, never a
single scope occupied at a time | | think more of these spaces than
at the full, simply pulled over forest | | go sparsely into that intensity
of attribution

James McLaughlin

[untitled]

1.
The sounds from the water were unhappy with us.
Let me do your bidding and do not hurry –
said an incline.

On the copper field wrought with insect
and jewel.
They were alone:
substance and time – rays set on a non-zero vector –
applied to the long grass –
to each variable complex,
together fleeting with no elision

What is structural here in this violet choir?
All is too familiar; too precise.
Mathematically we are made pure –
of complex numbers and factors –
just at the heart of the soul.

Not

Approximate to our intentions,
contrite limitation –
At this distance and ineptitude
In the insolate equality -

2.
a lull a still
moment into moment
movement into movement
some sweep over the bleaching dune

dead
lethargy – what other options
the old stained reflection
that fails into silence.

was it God in this river
this ochre sun
a semantic cry or yell for help
our pleximetry notes are quiet
the subjugated breath benignant

not from thriving

all cools

in quality and substance
towards a trickle

3.
of water ... this sunken myth that we lived.
Its now. An inane billow.
hear it shhh...
It's tracks ... The ashen memory of the woods.
The stone buttercups dance on our passion.

What are we. So often.
The ceramic mirror like a truth, that melted
in the ice.
Do you recall the red leaves.
We fell in its afterbirth, knowing how little we cared.

Imagination loved us. We knew.
We walked the dead dreams. We died.
And rose again. We pushed back stones.
In sandpits. In the infinite euphony of fellowship.

Do you remember it. I do.
Ascertained in every charm. Daylight.
Oh and those flowers everywhere. So yellow
Everywhere is fragrance.

And all was observed in reverence. Taken in
tetonic, mellifluous. The dead heroes.
And the curiosity of forever. We got softheaded with it.
The pulseless eyes twist us back in a line.

Diane Mulholland

You Asked Me if God was Real

And while I was considering my answer, a solitary bee
flew inside my open mouth and made her nest.
She laid an egg and packed it deftly in a case. Then six more,
in a row along my stifled tongue, before she flew away.

I held them there and thought of daisies, of fresh-cut grass,
and summer wine. And by the time September came
any words I might have spoken were not needed.
All I did was stand still as seven tiny, perfect bees broke free
and balanced for a moment on my lips to dry their wings.

The Three Angels, or,
How We Found What We Truly Wanted

The first angel came to us limping. The wound in her heel was edged
with black and the poison crept upwards, drawing with it a map of
her stretched and screaming veins. The surgeons caught up scalpels
but when they cut into the flesh and saw that the angel's bones were
made of purest silver they laid aside their saws for who could destroy
such beauty?

The second angel clutched her side but the slash was too broad and
blood ran through her fingers. Where it dripped and soaked into the
earth, green shoots sprang up and we were delighted at them and
followed the stream as flowers bloomed along it. We plucked vivid
bouquets and used them to buy favours and power for ourselves.

Still hungry, we went looking for the third angel, and found her
hanging high at the top of a tree. Her robes were star-bright and
their warmth stirred the scent of pine and drew us into the branches.
Coloured lights dazzled all around us as we climbed higher and when

we couldn't get close enough to her outstretched arms to be satisfied
we hung ourselves to be more like her. And our faces turned blue
like hers and our protruding tongues flapped out our message to the
rest of the world.

The Five Sisters

after a painting by Pablo Picasso

I have heard that there was only one woman,
one of Picasso's lovers, who posed for him again and again,
getting sharper and crosser each time. If this is true,
the five minds behind the five faces
may or may not all have the same opinions.

I didn't want to carry a poster tube through the streets,
so in the gift shop I chose a postcard. It was too small.
Only by bringing the point of my nose right up to the cardboard
could I get anything from the picture. So I bought five wooden dolls –
my very own demoiselles – and posed them around my bedroom,
little angled legs dangling off tops of bookcases.

They answered my questions just like sisters might.
'How do I know my soulmate?'
>   marry money
>   why marry at all?
>   you're too attached to your work
>   go with the boy next door
>   clock's ticking you know
'You're not giving me the right answers!'

I gathered them up and put them in a row along a shelf
and stood in front of them. 'Tell me, where do I find God?'
They laughed, their tiny, tinny voices ringing around the room.

I turned their backs on me, let them bump their knees and noses
on the spines of books. I got into bed with arms and legs held straight
under the tightly-tucked sheet. I tried to dream a road
but I couldn't see anything at all through their chattering.

Luke Palmer

This pen is a facsimile

of the original pen burnt
before the submission had dried.

The pen wrote several lines of varying proportions
from which this pen has been 3D printed.

This pen is a tool but not in the way a hammer
or a scalpel is a tool. It's more like a bag.

This pen remembers the interior spaces
that pens, bag-like, had hitherto surrounded.

This is all heavily ironic.
No one uses pens anymore.

There isn't even a pen here.

Wetmatter Phenomenon

This is the sky's translation of wetness, unfolding water
to show what it might mean to us now.
It reflects the modern condition
and our preoccupation with being wet.

It should not aid our cognition of the saturated state
but aims to commute our understanding
of what wetness has meant throughout its evolution
to a new paradigm.

Operating in a higher sphere than the original
this will touch us, fall on us, but never

will it make us truly wet.
It is not true water.

It is not the embryo of river or lake or sea
but a rephrasing. It shows the whole narrative of wetness
but it remains wetness's afterlife.
It can only suggest deluge or soaking or flood.

This therefore is an attempt
– our age's most complete attempt –
to reframe historic wetness
transcending any sensory index.

Yogesh Patel

Hope

They planted the bones in this desert
And hoped for the trees

The rain never spoke here with
The tap-dancing on barren roads
They are the words children won't hear
Yes, the tears may rain
But the trees won't grow

History never had a heart, just rubble
The future has a tail, coils, runs away
The birds are the circling Mig-29s
Cloud-tails scratching a silver-line

Damask Roses have fallen to dust
In the only monsoon where bullets rain
The hands that can farm are bones
In barbarians' metal-mushroom farms

The buzzards are the circling Mig-29s
Their cloud-tails drag a smoky silver-line
Puffed straight from a hookah by an old man
A wish: the man-made clouds will rain
One day
Where they planted the bones in this desert
And hoped for the trees

Aidan Semmens

In a Holy Place

the ruin is uninhabited
except by a seemingly ancient
wooden statue of the virgin

odd visions of maybe familiar
people on an unfamiliar street
an altar to the unknown goddess

illustrations of bewildering plants
charts of impossible heavens
female figures in a heavy hand

their postures and activities
having no parallel
in words or their erasure

the agents of conformity
pound highway and byway, not all
their weaponry metaphorical

in this brick structure great families
holy men and mystics meet
women with the saintliest of looks

Brueghel and Dürer study alchemy and law
clocks and musical instruments
in neat but unreadable glyphs

penned into tight cryptographic circles
the manuscript sold at a humiliating price
now available online, alien

fighter pilots and tank commanders
need to focus quickly
on all this corrugated dereliction

coming from an urban neighbourhood
places you in a higher category of risk
where it's not wealth that counts, but change

no one ever launched a war for numbers
and logic won't do it
we need a story, a moral decocted

from the most limited evidence
simple words in a half-formed language
sinister analysis of ritual codes

or perhaps, satirically, vice versa
musicians and enthusiasts, ghosts
at the soft edges of consciousness

mission creep and collateral damage
sipped from exotic, esoteric glasses
in bunkers that may not be secure

beneath their breath, hands holding
red and black cards, the ace of wands
gently waving in a breeze

the cover is blank, the water nymph
and virgin faintly seen, or perhaps
to read it this way is to miss the point

We Will Speak of This Again

to a certain extent all seaside places
resemble one another
the pleasureseekers depart
with the first cold autumnal storm

they nevertheless preserve unchanged
their forefathers' primitive habits of dress
their costumes exceedingly odd and amusing
their lives toilsome and cheerless

lined with quaint and picturesque
mediaeval buildings and that fatal field
where the modern mingles
with ancient gaiety, splendour and woe

before the rude cabins
rise frequently tall foul posts
carved from top to bottom
into grotesque resemblances

with their unintelligible decorations
and letterings and mysterious dark rooms
the combination of monotonous monosyllables
slip from the memory like drops of water

the entire audience smokes
and the performance goes on amid hideous
beating of drums and gongs
the gambling dens and opium cellars

should be visited in company
of a policeman and pilgrim troops
in tenement houses of men dozing
in half-drugged sleep

in this paradise inhabited by devils
it is clatteringly difficult to imagine
how a photographer ever contrived
to represent the street as tranquil

for civilisation is immeasurably
to be preferred to despotism
and here the hallowed waters are lined
with temples and booths where idols are sold

Valeria Melchioretto

Blood Moon

Follow your inner moonlight; don't hide the madness. —*Allen Ginsberg*

We sailed the Ocean of Storms on a wooden spoon with a dishcloth sail.
Waves were as tall as tradition, as hefty as the decades that set us apart.

Luckily no logbook survives so we now think it as the Sea of Tranquillity
for the moon feeds on madness and make-believe in order to wax and wean.

We also insist the moon landing actually happened how else could we go on?
That motherly moon had to be conquered so mankind could make that
            giant leap.

Men claim and defile that virgin sphere high above by planting a crude flag
so we won't be tempted to trespass or forget our rightful place on this earth.

But tonight I call you away from the kitchen sink to point at the night sky
For tonight the moon menstruates on a scale only a dead stones can bleed

because tonight moon and sun, past and always align with our delusions.
Our milky dreams are clearer and we both see the maternal is but a veil.

All lines up with our female lineage, a heritage I so carelessly squandered.
Yet sticky blood not only binds us together it also guides us through life,

it rules us the way sailors rely on a tide table to navigate rough waters
that wordless flow beyond data so badly misunderstood, over and over.

In an aim to reach that Terra Vitae, you and I eclipse in a bloody duty.
You seem to accept I had to follow my moonlight to its ultimate madness

while I perceive how madly you tried to turn into Venus of Willendorf
each time the moon was full, each time the gateway to history lit up.

Together we stand and gaze as if the sun could rise twice in a single day
as the bluer light simply scatters at the deepest depth of our womanly well.

Pimpinellifolia, Rosewood by No Other Name
For N. T.

Countless times you told me how on my birthday in mid-May
snowflakes fell as large as pristine white rose petals to mark

the Summer of Love although I was largely clueless about love
and your summers stayed bloomless like those of a beautiful shrub.

Crucially you gave away your power to bloom like your gift to me:
that ornate rosewood sewing kit oozing a scent to remember you by.

It had cryptic Cyrillic captions and was festooned with red flowers.
But unlike real rosebuds they never wilted and the thorns grew inward.

It was filled with needles and safety pins in all shapes and sizes
ready to darn right through each waking hour, set to mend every flaw.

A tall task even for spinsters born from stoic stock, off-spring
of survivors resilient enough to endure all and the bubonic plague.

How can I complain about those frostbitten summer's days when
your long black hair, your pale complexion and your painted roses

were so much like a fairytale, I could have cried myself to adulthood.
Now that I had my seven years of dog roses and a few odd baccaras

I see that you never had a prince but called a saucepan a saucepan,
a plastic bucket a plastic bucket and no void abstracts crossed your lips.

Your door was always open, always poised to step through as if into life,
as if into death, a door like a needle's eye, keen to thread a new day.

Summer is on its way out as your hair has turned from charcoal to ash
And even I have reached an age reserved to primroses and rosehip tea.

They no longer compare our eyes or noses or chins to point out a kinship,
and soon they will compare our ills, our aches, our ability to suffer well.

Your wildness cannot fit into walled gardens, you are so *pimpinellifolia*,
seasons are just a passing circumstance with no importance whatsoever.

Gerry Stewart

Invocation Against Winter

Unravel the skeins of geese
and lash them to the green fields.

Hold back the mushrooms' bloom,
warn the winds not to rise.

Blaze your bonfires on all shores,
their flames washing away night.

Till the earth with ashes of spruce
and birch to warm its depths.

Eat only fresh picked peas and berries,
fight the wasps for your share.

Build up the löyly★ in your sauna
until you burn clean all doubts.

Whip yourself raw with branches,
hot blood raised to the surface.

Drench yourself in the freezing lake,
alive in the glittering waves.

Pinpoint with your dart when the sun
arches high, dripping with honey.

Close your eyes and whisper three times,
se on kesä, se on kesä, se on kesä.

★*Finnish: literally 'steam' or 'heat,' but it refers more to the atmosphere
and mood of a sauna*

Gravity's Anchor

Wings curved, frozen in flight,
a songbird wind-fallen
amongst bruised apples.
Sweet-rot wraps around us.

Cradled in my child's hand,
its hardened body
seeks release. We too wish
to be weightless again.
Confined to a hard-packed grave
would be the final insult.

We stumble to leave it
in the deep woods
for the flies and foxes,
returned to the circle.
Trace its downy head,
whisper soft goodbyes.

Kicking leaves on the walk back,
a heavy procession,
we balance their questions
with our own doubts.

Louise Tondeur

After leaving you

The flat is full of your sleep. Like Bagpuss, everything sleeps with you. In the laundry basket, brown jeans, tracksuit bottoms, that top with the heart I bought from Target in Minneapolis, the one you don't like, knickers, my snoopy beach towel, fourteen years old: they act like odd fruit, spilling out onto the carpet, all asleep. Your suitcase, the batik of Saraswati that your friend brought back from Agra, book after book after book: all slumbering, leaning on each other's shoulders. Your dressing gown, torn and blue, is curled up beside me like a cat, rising and falling, breathing on its own, and Glen, the heater you bought with DO NOT COVER under the name like a clever slogan, white and beautiful, is asleep too. He's a new arrival, hasn't seen or heard or tasted anything, he is only ever hot or cold. The TV with the dog that you won in a raffle. Our clothes, not dry yet, drying together, shirts holding hands like we're not supposed to, although we keep forgetting. Candles, camomile tea in a mug bought at the top of the Cairngorms, plant, fan, futon, chest, photo, vase, bookshelf, carpet, walls, train ticket, letter, diary, cushions. All asleep: dreaming, turning, snorting, rubbing their eyes, banging their pillows, curling up like dormice, rehearsing lines to say in the daytime, playing out what they did yesterday and the day before. You've got flu. I made you soup. You were so hot it startled me: fiery, exhausted, scared and now asleep, like Bagpuss, pink and ragged. *Heat* magazine, a box from Office World, a ticking alarm clock, a wastepaper basket, coasters, remote control, hand-held hoover, more letters, photo albums, lights, weights, toaster, doors, old tan kettle, shoes, paint pot

Things you are afraid of

a sock from the kitchen floor a twenty pound note with blood on it a leaf inside the air conditioning jeans that have been on the train muddy paw prints on the skin pants that seagulls have shat on underwear cats put their tails on a blood spot in the bathroom cup that once had Calpol in it taking pills a way of lying in bed of opening and closing doors leaving doors open cleaning keys water-damaged washing machines hand-wringing in front of absent sinks letters that go unspoken word spells evoking forbidden places TV shows that go unwatched dogs unstroked painkiller diaries unreliable narrators terrible diseases wet water interrogation about bins that may or may not have been touched by red paint bird poo abandoned drinks and pyjamas that have touched the carpet where the cat has walked into fox noses and cobwebs on trousers swallowing cherry stones and cyanide choking on needles from the kitchen floor twenty pound sock with blood on it a note inside the air conditioning a leaf that has been on the train muddy jeans prints on the skin paws that pants have shat on seagulls cats put their tails on an underwear spot in the blood cup that once had a bathroom in it Calpol for taking pills the ritual of opening and closing bed leaving doors open cleaning doors water-damaged keys hand-wringing in front of absent washing machines letters that go unspoken sink spells evoking forbidden words TV shows that go places unwatched and unstroked dog diaries unreliable painkillers terrible narrators wet diseases interrogation about water that may or may not have been touched red bins or bird paint abandoned poo pyjamas that have touched the drinks where the carpet has walked into cat noses and foxes in trousers swallowing cyanide and cobwebs choking on cherry stones from the kitchen a blood sock washing machine unwatched dogs painted jeans unspoken diaries unreliable narrators terrible diseases

Dmitry Kedrin

translated by **Alex Cigale**

The Master Builders

Soon as the sovereign vanquished
The Golden Horde at Kazan',
He ordered his courtiers
To hire building masters.
And the benefactor commandeth –
So sayeth the words of the chronicler –
To commemorate the aforesaid victory
They would build a shrine of stone.

And they brought him
Florentines,
And Germans,
And the other
Men of foreign lands,
That drained wine goblets in a single breath.
And two came onto him,
Masons of Vladimir,
Two nameless Russian architects,
Handsome,
Barefooted,
Youthful.

Light poured into tiny silicate windows,
And the breath of the nobility was stale.
The tiled Russian stove.
The sanctuary.
The smoke and the heat.
And in homespun shirts
Before Ivan the Fourth,
Holding on tightly to each other's hands
Stood the masters.

"Peasants!
Can you erect me a church
That will be more beauteous
Than the foreign churches, I ask you?"
Having shook their hair off their foreheads
The masons replied:
"We can!
Order and it will be done, Master!"
And they fell at the Tsar's feet.
The sovereign so ordered.
And on Saturday of Holy Week,
Their hair pulled back with belts,
Crossing themselves at sunrise,
The sovereign's masons
Hastily donned their aprons
And on their broad shoulders
Carried bricks upon raw logs.

The masters wove
Patterns out of stone lace,
Erecting the columns
And, proud of their labors,
Burnished the dome with gold,
Covered the roofs' surface with azure
And inserted scales of glass
Inside the leaden frames.

And already the little archers' towers
Were stretching towards the heavens.
Traverses,
Little balconies,
Onion domes to the cupola.
And the learned people marveled,
For this church
Was prettier than all the Italian villas
And all the Indian pagodas!

The temple was miraculous,
All illumined by religious daubers.

At the altar,
And in the entrances,
And in the tsar's own gallery.
By the painting workshop
Of the monk Andrey Rublev
Decorated richly
In the strict Byzantine style....

And at the foot of the edifice
The market plaza buzzed,
Screaming unstintingly to the merchants:
"Show us, what you live by!"
At night, the crude folk
Drank in their mugs to kingdom come,
And in the morning howling in despair,
Repented and begged absolution.

The thief, flogged raw by the lash,
Lay by the scaffold not breathing,
The forelock of his grey beard pointing
Directly at the heavens,
And the Tatar khans,
Emissaries of the Golden Horde,
Trammelers of the Black Horde,
Languished in their Moscow servitude.

And above all this shame
That church stood
As a bride!
And in her sackcloth,
With a little turquoise ring in her mouth,
The carnal, coarse girl,
Stood by the Execution Square
And, in amazement,
Ogled at that beauty,
As at a fairy tale....

And when the temple was illumined,
With a staff in hand,

Wearing a monk's klobuk,
The tsar made the rounds of it –
From the cellars and sanctuaries
To the cross on the altar.
And having taken in with his gaze
Its patterned towers,
The Tsar proclaimed it "Beauteous!"
And all averred: "Beauteous!"

And the benefactor asketh:
"And could you make me another,
More graceful, more lovely
Than this cathedral?"
Having shook out their forelocks,
The masons replied,
"We can, Master!
Order, and it will be done!"

And they fell at the Tsar's feet.
And then the sovereign
Commandeth that the masons be blinded,
So that on all his lands
Such a church
Stand without equal,
That in Suzdal's lands
And in Ryazan'a demesne,
And in all the others
No better temple be erected,
Than the Temple of the Intercession!

Their falcon-like eyes
Were put out with an iron awl,
That they may never see
The light of day again.
And they branded them with branding iron,
And whipped them with switches painful,
And they threw them,
Unseeing,
On the cooled bosom of the earth.

And in the Market food stalls,
There, where the tavern trash sang,
Where it stank of rotgut,
Where it was dark from steam,
Where the privy clerks hollered:
"The Lord's word is our bond!" –
They begged for bread and wine
For the sake of Christ our Master.

And their church stood
So beautiful
That it seemed as in a dream.
And its bells rang
As though it were mourning them,
And the forbidden song
Of the terrible mercy of the Tsar
Was sung in the secret places
By gusli players everywhere
Across all of wide Russia.

1938

Christ and the Foundry Worker

Master blacksmith Grachev,
Surrounded by barrels of scrap,
And the cupola furnace simmers,
And the viscous smelt is dense.
The heavy doors swing open
And five usnskilled workers
Roll a Christ into the room
On a rough-hewn dolly cart.
He lies there, like a dead log,
Before the angry humming cupola,
And, keeping a low profile, is silent,
Like a ram at market, under the knife.
On his head is a wreath of thorns,

On his fallen-in chest a gash.
And with a hammer, Grachev
Pounds on this green pig iron:

"You threatened me with hell,
Stole both my life and my work.
You promised me paradise
For my patience here on earth,
I do not believe a word you say.
I need neither heaven nor hell.
Prepare yourself, you deceiver;
Now, you too will taste of the pit!
Whether you like it or not,
You'll rescue us yet, you penny idol,
You will feed us with your flesh –
Your dense and viscous metal.
Having melted you down,
We will replace the nonferrous
Details of rail cars with your
Lighter, cheaper pig iron type.

The others wait with their cart nearby.
"Get him out of here!" Grachev tells them.
The muffled ringing of the rails,
And the furnace roiling to the brim.
"Sin yea not, oh, simple man!"
The savior cries out his deception.
"I will boil you in a pot, you little god!"
Grachev blurts a response right back.
And they carry the pig iron god
Towards the furnace, taking breaks,
Laughing all the while, and immerse him
In the cauldron's red-hot liquid.
His body is entirely submerged,

And only the Master's rail-thin arm,
Arranged to clench its missing cross,
Pokes through and out of the cupola.

He'd raised up the fingers of his hand,
Gaunt and pointy, to the heavens,
Preaching to the impoverished
Humility amidst the earthly sorrows,
Above the pregnant peasant woman,
Above the sickly scurvied infant,
Above the Jewish pogrom's bloodbath,
Above gallows, above strife, above war.

The master smith paces the grounds,
Pouring in some sand, now and then
Skimming away the frothy scum,
And the orange froth grows rarer.
"Take away your rotten arm!"
Grachev scolds the boiling god.
And the cauldron seethes,
And the arm vanishes...

Vanishes for the ages!
Taking a swing at the deceitful god
With his full force the human being
Strikes with an iron sledge hammer
So that along with the Redeemer,
We as well forever forget the path
Toward our pure and bright earth,
And the gallows, and the pogrom.

The channel steel foundry drowns
In a racket, the assembly chatters
And shrieks, the hydraulics rumble,
And the forge spits out steam –
It is the breathing of Industry,
The rail car foundry in Mytishchi,
Tensing and straining, it hums,
Expending its extenuating breach.

I have grown to love this hum,
Accustomed to its mechanical fury.

I sit down to rest on a stone
Between the sand bags filled with earth.
And Grachev comes over to me
And proposes: "Let's have us a smoke…"
Alright, comrade, let's take a smoke break
Then, while the God here percolates.

1932

The Finch

In spring, in the public garden, I captured a finch.
The bow and net trap snatched it in its wolf's jaw.
A singer of the woods, he was small and afraid,
But like a mighty hero, he met captivity in silence.

He'd grown accustomed to singing the wood's glory
Under the friendly sun on the tip of a sticky branch.
And so, no! His gilded song will not erupt in sound
Within the cramped confines of this wretched cage.

The stubborn one! He would not resemble us,
Sick people, drab, compliant, pliable and colorless;
Fluffing his crest feathers, he sullenly flared out,
My little prisoner, my proud and arrogant finch.

Not even a proffered palmful of succulent ant eggs
Would call forth the affirmation of his jubilant trill.
His sullen eyes gazed into those of my menagerie
Of domesticated birds with a measure of contempt.

He kept gazing out to the field beyond the window
Through the dense thicket of the wire mesh net,
Until I covered him with a rough sackcloth,
To darken his lightly rocking and swaying cage.

1939

Maximilian Voloshin

translated by Alex Cigale

War

1.
Peace hath dominion.
The nations, satiated,
Revelled: satisfied with themselves,
Their material abundance, their general amity.
And only rarely, exchanging glances,
Did they pounce on the weakest and,
Swallowing him whole, growling, withdrew,
Their jaws scowling sideways,
Once again grown tranquil.
All things went well with the world:
A trillion cog wheels
Manipulated the hammers and the lever gears,
Forging the steel,
Boring the cannons,
The Chemist
Prepared the lyddite and the melinite,
The learned men invented a means
After a means for exterminating the masses,
Politicians surveyed the maps
Of new colonial routes and markets,
Thinkers scribbled about the general,
Undisruptable peace upon the land,
Women swayed in the grips of limber tango,
Baring the attractions of their powdered flesh.
The manometer of culture was approaching
The ultimate degree of crushing force.

2.
Just then, out of the nether depths,
Was heard a voice, proclaiming: "It is time

To stomp the wine press of fury. For out of
Demons sent to serve them,
People did fashion bodies
And erect thrones,
Giving the wrath of fire free rein
In the muzzles' acceleration
And the compression of the projectile,
For having bestowed the muscle
Of running feet and the wheel's whirlwind
Onto the indifference of flowing waters
And humid fog, for having woven a nest
For the rebellious spirits of explosion
Within the wilful currents of the air,
Into the host of iron spiders,
Relentlessly weaving
Both suckling and suffocating webs –
For all of these, I discharge
The captive demons
From their oath of obedience, and chaos,
Constricted in the whirlwinds of substance,
From their structured order of music!
I grant them dominion over the earth
As long as people
Vanquish them not again having
Subdued and conquered within themselves
Anger, greed, willfulness, and indifference."

3.
And saw I this: the heaven's gates did open
In the constellation of Leo, and the demons
Flung themselves upon the earth…
People huddled together in the river vales
Signifying the boundaries of mighty kingdoms,
And having excavated in the earth
Tunnels, serpentine and murine passages,
They pastured herds of gluttonous monsters:
Themselves both pastor and fodder.

4.

It was as though time itself was overturned,
And the world seemed alike onto
The unchristened waters of flood: gargantuan
Contorted serpents crawled out of the slime,
The iron spiders swarmed,
The asps did swallow lightning,
Dragons spewed forth
Shafts of flame and stung with their tails,
In rivers and in seas the fish
Spawned
Deadly roe,
From winged lizards
Light flared, explosive and fiery eggs
Poured down upon the earth,
And swarms of insects,
Monstrous in dimension and formation,
Implanted flaming maggots
In the bodies of men –
Having acquired from people
Wrath and lust and rage,
Stung the human flesh, clawing,
Tearing, crushing, searing, chewing, devouring,
And the cities, like millstones,
Turned tirelessly and milled
Their select grain
Out of each family's firstborn
To make demon feed.
And thousands of people
Flung themselves in inspired frenzy,
With joyfulness, under the rim of the wheel.
Nations, one after another,
Conjoined and twined into choirs
Under the clatter and clanging of machines,
And never was such dance of death
Seen before in this frenzied world!

5

Yet more! more! For nothing seemed to suffice...
And then another cry resounded: "Away with
War between tribes, and armies, and front lines:
Long live the cause of Civil War!"
And armies, having mingled their ranks, in rapture,
Did kiss the enemies' cheeks, and then,
Flinging themselves on their kin, chopping and killing,
Executed by firing squad, hung, put them to torture,
Feeding upon human flesh,
Pickling the children away for future use –
There was devastation, and famine.
And finally came the plague.

6.

A sightless time now dawned upon the earth,
The world seemed wider, somehow more spacious,
For now, there were fewer men,
But for these too,
Among the wastelands, room was insufficient,
And they became inflamed only after one thing,
To sooner build yet more machines
To resume the same war yet again.
This skirmish, delirious, came to an end,
But in this slaughter they grasped nothing,
And from all this learned was not a thing.

January 29, 1923, Koktobel

The Terror

They mustered up for work at night. Read out
    The denunciations, affidavits, "cases".
Hurriedly signed the verdicts, passed sentences.
    Dithered and yawned. Drank beer.

In the morning, they started plying the soldiers
    With vodka. In the evening, by candlelight,
They called out the men and women from the list,
    Rounding them up together in an unlit yard.

They removed their shoes, clothes, underwear
    And, tying these together in bundles,
Loaded them on carts and, having carted them off,
    Divvied the rings and watches left behind.

At night, they herded them, shoeless and naked,
    Along the ice-cold paving stones,
Under the stiff northeastern wind, to wastelands
    And vacant lots beyond the city.

They forced them with rifle butts to the cliff's edge.
    In the beams of handheld flashlights,
The machine guns went to work for a half minute.
    They finished them off with bayonets.

Those still living were shoveled into pits,
    Hurriedly covered over with dirt.
And then with rolling rounds of Russian song
    They returned, to city and home.

As daylight broke, wives, mothers, hungry hounds
    Made their way towards the same ravines
And, digging up the dirt with their bare hands,
    Scuffled for the bones, and kissed dear flesh.

April 26, 1921, Simferopol

Famine

Bread is of the earth, but famine is from people:
They've sown it with the bodies of the executed,
Shoots sprouting forth in the shape of grave crosses,
And the earth has germinated no other nurslings.
The harvest hidden, requisitioned, taken away,
Levies collected in bread, they confiscated even
The household cattle, and the very seed grain.
The peasants went out to plant in the dark of night.

In autumn, along with the nuthatches, starving people
Crawled out like lowly earthworms along the streets.
At the bazaars, inflamed throngs flared up for bread.
They threw the thief down to the ground, kicked him
In the face, and he, hiding his head in the dirt,
Still struggled to ingest that crust of a loaf butt…
Like exterminating starlings, they shot the gangs
Of boys gleaning grain along the country lanes,
And these blackened lumps of coal littered the way
In frozen heaps stiffened with rubbish and nut shells.

The earth was nauseated by corpses – lying about
In the streets, emitting a stench in the mortuaries,
Rotting in open pits at all the cemeteries.
In gullies and garbage dumps, skeletons
Lay scattered, their soft flesh sliced off.
Curs gnawed upon arms and heads torn off.
Hawkers at the markets were doing a lively trade:
Cheap jellied meat for sale, nauseating sausage.
There was sheep to be had for three hundred,
And the human flesh, for only forty rubles.
The soul had long been cheaper than the flesh,
And the mothers who had slaughtered their children
Salted them for future use: "I gave birth by myself
and I will eat by myself… I can give birth to another"…

The starving were making love and giving birth
To screaming crimson pieces of senseless meat:
Without joints, without gender, without eyes.
Ulcerations born out of the stench,
Out of the horror of the commonplace.
And the delirium of the sick was less crazed
Than the habitation of these bed sheets and pots.

When through the winter gloom the spring curdled
Above this pus-filled pestilence of humanity
And the flame raced with its tongues
The breadth of the fields and the height of the naked
Twigs, its sweet fragrance seemed an affront,
The light of the sun, a mockery, and flowers, sacrilege.

1923

Notes on Contributors

MICHAEL AIKEN is a poet from Sydney, Australia. His first book, *A Vicious Example*, was published by Grand Parade Poets in 2014 and was subsequently shortlisted for the NSW Premier's Kenneth Slessor Prize for Poetry, the Dame Mary Gilmore Prize and an Australian Book Design Award. His second book, the verse novella, *Satan Repentant* (UWA Press, 2018), was written under the mentorship of David Malouf as part of the *Australian Book Review*'s inaugural Laureate's Fellowship.

JONATHAN CATHERALL has published work in *Blackbox Manifold, Molly Bloom, Tears in the Fence, Envoi, Datableed, 3AM, Epizootics!* and others. He has reviewed for a range of publications, and edits the quarterly online magazine *Tentacular.* (www.tentacularmag.com)

ALEX CIGALE's own poems in English appear in *Colorado Review, The Common Online*, and *The Literary Review*, and his translations of classic and contemporary Russian poetry in *Harvard Review Online, Kenyon Review Online, Modern Poetry in Translation, New England Review, PEN America, Plume, TriQuarterly, The Hopkins Review, Two Lines, Words Without Borders,* and *World Literature in Translation.* In 2015, he was awarded an NEA Fellowship in Literary Translation for his work on the poet of the St. Petersburg philological school, Mikhail Eremin, and guest-edited the Spring 2015 Russia Issue of the *Atlanta Review*. His first full book, *Russian Absurd: Daniil Kharms, Selected Writings* came out in the Northwestern University Press World Classics series in 2017.

CLAIRE CROWTHER has three collections and a chapbook from Shearsman, with a new full-length collection, *Solar Cruise*, in the works. She lives in Somerset, and is co-editor of *Long Poem Magazine*.

CATHY DREYER is a poet and critic who lives near Wantage in Oxfordshire. Her examination of Carrie Etter's *Imagined Sons* and Ted Hughes's *Birthday Letters* is shortly to appear in a special edition of Intellect's *Journal of Writing in Creative Practice.*

KERRY FEATHERSTONE teaches at Loughborough University, and was the 2017-2018 Poet in Residence at Bradgate Park, Leicestershire.

AMLANJYOTI GOSWAMI's collection of poems, *River Wedding*, was published by Poetrywala in March this year. His poems have been published in India, Nepal, Hong Kong, the UK, USA, South Africa, Kenya and Germany, including the anthologies, *40 under 40: An Anthology of Post Globalisation Poetry* (Poetrywala) and *A Change of Climate* (Manchester Metropolitan University, Environmental Justice Foundation and the University of Edinburgh). His poems have also appeared on street walls of Christchurch, exhibitions in

Johannesburg and buses in Philadelphia. He grew up in Guwahati, Assam and lives in Delhi.

NORMAN JOPE has three collections, one of them, *Dreams of the Caucasus*, from Shearsman Books. He lives in Plymouth and was editor of *Memes*.

DMITRY KEDRIN (1907-1945), a second generation Russian Modernist, remains almost entirely unknown in the English language. That this master craftsman was almost certainly murdered is not what makes him the ideal subject for this miniature study in literary history. While Kedrin's very substantial gift spanned both lyrical and dramatic poetry; he is perhaps best known, and most interesting for, dwelling in myth and history, his work with folk and epic materials. Though he published only a single slim volume in his lifetime, the 1940 *Witnesses* (17 poems), he was influential, much read and admired, including for his translations (from Bashkir, Balkar, Tatar, Ukrainian, Lithuanian and Belorussian), and published widely in the periodical press. In addition to his civic lyrics from the beginning of WWII included here, he is best known for the first poem (1938). 'Zodchie' (Master Builders) retells the story of Ivan the Terrible, who had the architects of St. Basil's Cathedral blinded to prevent them from recreating their masterpiece. The poem was widely perceived as a deliberate, conscious (and conscientious) attempt to directly address the current tyrant. Stalin's personal animus casts a long shadow over Kedrin's lack of book publication, and ultimately, over the untimely "cause of his death". Dmitry Kedrin died on the night of September 18, 1945 when he was thrown from a train platform, in a second, successful attempt on his life.

PETER LARKIN has several volumes from Shearsman Books, most recently *Introgression Latewood*. A new collection is in preparation.

MARY LEADER has published four collections, the most recent of which is *She Lives There Still* (Shearsman Books, 2018). Now retired from teaching, she lives in Oklahoma.

JOHN LEVY lives in Tucson, Arizona. "I have had the pleasure of being published in *Shearsman* previously. I am submitting again because I like the magazine." [And what John doesn't say here is that he was involved with the magazine at its very beginnings in 1981...].

JAZMINE LINKLATER has published the pamphlets *Toward Passion According* (Zarf, 2017) and *Découper, Coller* (Dock Road Press, 2018). She works for T-Junction International Poetry Festival and Carcanet Press, and co-organises *No Matter*, a new experimental reading series in Manchester. She is one of three poets chosen by *Poetry London* for mentoring in 2018-19, and is mentored by Vahni Capildeo.

DS Maolalaí recently returned to Ireland after four years away, now spending his days working maintenance dispatch for a bank and his nights looking out the window and wishing he had a view. His first collection, *Love is Breaking Plates in the Garden*, was published in 2016 by Encircle Press in New England. He has twice been nominated for the Pushcart Prize.

Ruth McIlroy has been published in *The Poetry Review, The Rialto,* and *The North*, and in anthologies produced by Templar and The Poetry Business, among others. She has been placed in various competitions including The York Literary Festival Poetry Competition and The Philip Larkin West Riding Poetry Competition.

She won the 2017 Poetry Business Book and Pamphlet Competition, and her winning pamphlet *Guppy Primer* was the Poetry Book Society Pamphlet Choice for Winter 2017. She read at the launch of the Spring 2018 *Poetry Review.*

James McLaughlin has been in these pages on several previous occasions. He lives in Dumbarton, Scotland, and has published three collection with Knives, Forks and Spoons Press: *Justified Sonnets, Aeido* and *Text 1.*

Julie Maclean lives on the Surf Coast, Australia. She is the author of *Lips That Did* (Dancing Girl Press, Chicago, 2017), *To Have To Follow*, a collaboration with Terry Quinn (Indigo Dreams, 2016), *Kiss of the Viking* (Poetry Salzburg, 2014), *You Love You Leave* (Kind of a Hurricane Press, USA, 2014) and *When I saw Jimi* (Indigo Dreams, 2013). Website: juliemacleanwriter.com

Valeria Melchioretto is the author of *Podding Peas* and *The End of Limbo*. She won the Writing Ventures Competition in 2005 and received an Arts Council bursary. She is a Hawthornden Fellow. In 2012 she represented Switzerland at the Poetry Olympics. She holds a MA in Creative Writing from Birkbeck, and her short collection *1348 & Other Equations* is due out soon from Eyewear Publishing.]

Diana Mulholland is a poet and essayist. She was born in rural Australia and moved to London with her husband in 2006. Her work has appeared in several online and print journals including *The Interpreter's House, Brittle Star,* and *Under the Radar*, and in 2017 she was highly commended in both the Bristol Poetry Prize and the Manchester Cathedral Poetry Prize.

A former primary-school teacher, Diane is currently studying for an MA in Creative Writing at Manchester Metropolitan University and is working towards her first full collection.

Luke Palmer is a recent graduate of the MA programme at Bath Spa University and has placed work with (among others) *Agenda, The Interpreter's House, The Cardiff Review* and *The Tangerine.*

Yogesh Patel runs the *Word Masala Project* to promote writers and poets of the South Asian diaspora. He also edits *eSkylark*. He writes a regular column for *Confluence*. Additionally, Yogesh is a founder of the literary charity, Gujarati Literary Academy, and has served as its president. He was a Fellow of the International Poetry Society and a Fellow of the Royal Society of Arts. He was awarded the Freedom of the City of London and, as a trilingual poet, has four LP records, two films, radio programmes, children's books, fiction and non-fiction books, as well as poetry collections to his credit.

Apart from being a recipient of the IWWP award, the International Scottish Diploma for excellence in poetry, and an Honorary Diploma from the Italian University of Arts, he has won the Co-Op Award for poetry on the environment. By profession, Yogesh is a qualified optometrist and an accountant.

Simon Perchik is a retired attorney whose poems have appeared in *Partisan Review, Forge, Poetry, Osiris, The New Yorker* and elsewhere. His most recent collection is *The Osiris Poems* published by boxofchalk in 2017. For more information, including free e-books and his essay 'Magic, Illusion and Other Realities', see his website at www.simonperchik.com. To view one of his interviews go to: https://www.youtube.com/watch?v=MSK774rtfx8

Peter Robinson published his *Collected Poems* with Shearsman Books in 2017. He is a Professor at the University of Reading.

David Rushmer is a librarian at Cambridge University. His first full-length collection, *Remains to Be Seen*, was published by Shearsman Books in 2018.

Aidan Semmens is the author of four poetry collections, *A Stone Dog* (2011), *The Book of Isaac* (2013), *Uncertain Measures* (2014) and *Life Has Become More Cheerful* (2017), three of them from Shearsman. He is also the editor of *By The North Sea: an anthology of Suffolk poetry* (Shearsman Books, 2013) and of the online poetry magazine *Molly Bloom*.

For several years he was a weekly columnist for the *Ipswich Star* and the *Eastern Daily Press*. He has been wielding a lens since 1965; his photos have appeared in various newspapers, magazines and academic books.

Vik Shirley is a poet from Bristol. Her poems have appeared in *Queen Mob's Teahouse, Zarf Poetry, Stride Magazine, Shearsman, The Interpreter's House* and in the *Dostoevsky Wannabe Cities: Bristol* pamphlet. A poem of hers was commended in the Verve Poetry Competition 2018 and published in the associated city poems anthology, *It All Radiates Outwards*. She has an MA in Creative Writing from Bath Spa University.

Gerry Stewart is a poet, creative writing tutor and editor based in Finland. Her poetry collection *Post-Holiday Blues* was published by Flambard Press. Her writing blog can be found at http:/thistlewren.blogspot.fi/.

LOUISE TONDEUR was born in Poole in 1972, and grew up in Bournemouth. She is a graduate of the MA in Creative Writing at the University of East Anglia, and was singled out as one of the most promising contributors to their *First Hand* anthology. Louise lives in Cambridge, and has published two novels and a collection of short stories.

MAXIMILIAN VOLOSHIN (1877–1932) – a second-generation Russian Symbolist poet, important translator of French Symbolist poetry, late-in-life world-class watercolourist and landscape artist – was a central figure of the Russian Silver Age. A selection of Alex Cigale's translations of his 'Inscriptions on Watercolors', which he had elevated into a unique hybrid poetic form in its own right, appeared in *Eleven Eleven* 14 (CCA). In 1909, Voloshin carried out one of the great literary hoaxes – the so-called Cherubina de Gabriak affair – that ended in a duel with Nikolay Gumilyov. Alex Cigale's translation of Voloshin's account of this was published in the *New England Review* 36.3 (2015). In the aftermath of the Russian Revolution, Voloshin's house and place of self-exile on the Crimean Peninsula became a temporary home and refuge for poets of all stripes and aesthetics, from Khlebnikov, to Gumilyov, Mandelstam, and Tsvetaeva. As it remains to this day, Crimea was one of the focal points of the Russian Civil War (1917-1922), and these are among the first poems to document the famine, starvation, and political terror that followed in its wake. Also of significance is that these are among the earliest poems to bear the stamp of Constructivism. They are a small selection from his little-known book, *The Terror*, published in Berlin in 1923.

PETRA WHITE is an Australian poet, born in Adelaide in 1975, and now living in London with her husband and daughter. Her first published collection of poetry, *The Incoming Tide*, was shortlisted for the Queensland Premier's Literary Awards and the ACT Poetry Prize. Her most recent collection is *A Hunger* (Melbourne: John Leonard Press).